L. F. Hackett

A Dream

And Other Poems

L. F. Hackett

A Dream
And Other Poems

ISBN/EAN: 9783744705424

Printed in Europe, USA, Canada, Australia, Japan

Cover: Foto ©Thomas Meinert / pixelio.de

More available books at **www.hansebooks.com**

A DREAM,

AND

OTHER POEMS.

BY

MISS L. F. HACKETT.

––––––––

CHICAGO.

1880.

CONTENTS:

PART I.

PART II.

PART I.

A DREAM.

I dreamed that I to heaven went,
And, being on an errand bent,
I hastened on, intent to find
An answer to the question in my mind,—
'Twas this: Do angels here employment find
For the body or for the mind?
As I stood gazing round about,
I saw a multitude, and heard a shout
Come from a vast, a mighty throng.
This was the burden of their song
(They were singing hymns of praise
To Him who hath no end of days):
"Glory be to God who sits on high!
Who unto us is ever nigh;

For he did send to us his own dear Son,

Through whose sufferings we have won,

And he saved us by his blood

As he did Noah from the flood."

And as I listened, tho' unseen,

I saw, far off upon a green,

What seemed to me another race.

So opposite were they in form and face;

So cheerful they, and happy too,

Not scared by any bugaboo;

Not singing long and doleful tune,

But gay as any bird in June;

Bright, too, as are the flowers in May.

Thinks I, that's the very place to stay,

Where I can merry be, and gay;

Yes, that I know will pay.

But first I thought I would inquire

And know to what I did aspire,—

Whether this people were as they did seem,

Of heavenly mind, sweet and serene.

But, to return to my first question,

Without waiting for dictation,

In front of that vast, that mighty throng,

Who now had finished up their song,

Sat one upon a great white throne,

Exalted high, tho' not alone,

Who now was giving loud command

To one who sat at his right hand.

"Watch well," said he, "these people now at leisure,

Lest they seek their own, not my, good pleasure;·

For they upon your merits come,

Relying not on any good which they have done,

But solely your great merits claim.

This sentiment I do disdain,

Knowing well man will take credit

For all in him that seems a merit;

And, while they hope to always rest,

They'll find that work for them is best,—

Work for the body as well as the mind;

Doing good to all mankind,

In the heavens above, and on the earth,—

Everywhere that man hath birth.

So watch them well, as I have said,

For they still think their sins on you are laid,

Which they will find a great mistake

After a few changes they shall make,—

After they shall have gone up higher,

And for all good they do aspire.

But cycles of ages shall run on

Ere their debts are canceled one by one,

Ere they to heavenly bliss attain,

Ere they are freed from earthly stain;

Then true happiness they will find

In lifting up, not casting down, their kind.

While to these people you attend
I'll seek those who always were my friend.
They never in their heart have said,
'God owes us debts he ne'er has paid;
Our way hedged up and pent
With bars o'er which we could not leap,
Left us our way to wend o'er mountain steep
With no kind hand to lead or guide
Or help us up the mountain side.'
Oh no; they say, 'He's been our friend
And ever will be to the end;
And Him we will adore,
Throughout all time and evermore.
Although by man condemned
To endless tortures with the damned,
We'll ever walk in wisdom's ways,
And to our God will give the praise,
Until we meet him far above,

Where all is peace, and joy, and love.'

I love them well, these people true;

They loyal are to me,—'true blue',—

And they no watching need;

Are not puffed up; not filled with greed.

They their fellow men did love,—

Were kind and gentle like a dove;

And, tho' to heaven they did aspire,

Did not consign their brother to hell-fire.

This myth they never did receive,

Because they neither could nor would believe

That God who made the world so fair

Would send men's souls to dark despair.

Now I let them play upon the green,

Surrounded by all things pleasant to be seen;

By flowers sweet, and rich, and rare,

Which they do often cull with care,

And carry down to earth, or send

With messages of love to friend.

They dwell in mansions bright and fair,

No longer cumbered with earthly care;

Their souls together sweetly blend,

While all their aspirations higher tend.

And they still seek the good of all,

Both high and low, both great and small:

This is the secret of their great content,

Which naught will ever here prevent."

Then, turning 'round to me, He said:

"Tho' their debts are not yet fully paid,

They'll always find some sweet employment;

And, if you like, can now make comment."

To this no answer I could make,

Feeling that I had much at stake;

So, musing awhile before I spoke,

I made an effort, and then awoke.

This is the moral I would teach:

Practice well before you preach;

Be not righteous in your own conceit,

Lest you find your heart full of deceit.

Depend not on another's merit;

Be pure in heart, and thus find credit.

While to heaven you desire to go,

Send not your brother to eternal woe.

Remember, God is good to all,

Whether they be great or small.

When from his hand you do receive

Good gifts, on him believe.

And while the paths of life you tread,

Forget not that the so-called dead

Are still alive and journeying on,

And you shall meet them one by one

In that bright world above,

Where all is harmony and love.

A HYMN.

There is a land, far, far above
  This earthly land of ours,
Filled with immortal love divine,
  Where ever bloom the flowers;
Where envy, discord or distrust
  Can never fill the breast,
For God, the Father, then will give
  To his beloved, rest.

Refreshing showers shall descend
  Upon the buds and flowers,
And fragrance ever fill the air,
  Fresh from the heavenly bowers,
While incense from the throne of God
  Shall rob the heart of care,—
Shall give the tired spirit rest
  And free from every snare.

Waft the heavenly breezes o'er me
    Till my tired spirit rests
Where earthly cares cannot oppress me
    And the weary find their rest;—
Where the angels stand awaiting,
    The new born spirit to receive;—
Where earthly sorrow then shall
    Nevermore disturb or grieve.

PRAYER.

I know not where to lay my aching head.
Where shall I lay the weary burden down?
How 'scape the chastening rod?
Help me to shun the paths of sin,
That tempt my still unwary feet.
Help me the immortal goal to win,
And may I henceforth enter in
To heavenly rest, and be forever blest.

DESTINY.

Thy way's maped out, and in it thou must go,
Whether it leads to summer flowers or winter snow;
So thou must patient be, whatever may betide,
As down the tide of life you slowly glide.
What tho' thy bed's not made of eider down,
Is that good reason why thy brow should wear a
    frown,
And though shouldst don the sable robe of discon-
    tent?
Then upward look and find that sweet content,—
That balm to weary souls, God's grace and love.
Be wise, be mild, be gentle like a dove;
Then shall thy life be peaceful as of yore,
And thou shalt learn for thee's laid up in store
A goodly heritage,—a mine of wealth; yea, more:
An eternity of blissful peace and joy,
Which naught can evermore disturb or cloy.

And now good bye until I again can greet thee;
At some convenient season I will meet thee.

You very soon shall find
Peace and comfort to your mind;
Then upward look, and be content
To know thy souls no longer rent
With discord or inharmony.

A CALL TO MISSIONARY WORK.

Among the countless millions there's but a chosen
few

To do the Master's bidding and his work again renew.

Then rise up in your manhood, and spread God's
banner high;

Shake out its folds of beauty against the broad blue
sky;

For on it now is written, in characters of gold,

The oft-repeated motto, which never can grow old,

"With no malice toward the erring, and with char-
ity for all,"

I will answer to the cry of my children when they
call.

Then help to raise thy brother, and his stubborn
will subdue,

By telling him the story, which he will find is true.

Tell him that God, the Father, doeth all things well,

Tho' ofttimes in the heart he seemeth not to dwell,

But so high above his creatures, in the heavens
above,

That he cannot stoop to bless them with his presence
or his love.

Oh! how we often err—we creatures of an hour—

In doubting God's great love, his wisdom and his
power.

Oh! raise the banner high; soon the victory will
be won,

And man shall be subdued and conquered one by
one.

As the hosts are marshalled up, their armor they'll
lie down;

And even as the cross they bore, so great shall be
their crown.

Then soar to loftier heights;

Uplift on eagle's wing;

Ascend the mountain of the Lord,

And to the breeze his banner fling.

FROM MY GUARDIAN SPIRIT.

When first I returned to this earth,
  A mission to me was given;
'Twas this: To lend my aid to you
  In making your way to Heaven.
Perhaps you find it a thorny road
  In which you have to travel,
But if you keep on, and never look back,
. The mystery you'll unravel.

The way may seem both gloomy and dark, ·
  And long may seem the journey.
If you could only rend the veil
  Your face would look less gloomy;—
Your eyes would sparkle with delight,
  Your heart be filled with bliss;—
Your face with radiant light would shine,
  And naught disturb your happiness.

LOOK WITHIN.

All nature wears her brightest hues.
The earth, the sea, the sky,
All speak the great Creator, God,
To be forever nigh.
The moon looks down with kindly face,
And sees poor mortals strive;
The sun looks, too, upon the scene,—
Sees erring mortals fail to give
Each other credit due.
Ah! short of sight; yea, blind,—
Ye mortals filled with sin.
Why seek ye not the narrow path,
Nor the immortal goal to win,
Ere the heart grows hard and callous too
By slighting conscience' call?
Oh! turn, poor erring mortal, turn,
While yet the Master calls,
Before it be too late.

RESIGNATION.

It was a fearful night, and all around looked dark.

The waves dashed high against my small, frail bark.

Oh! how I prayed, that weary night,

For strength, for wisdom, and for might

To do the work that God would have me do.

No answer came unto my prayer,

Until I gave up all that I held dear,—

Friends, kindred, home, and seeming honor too.

Then came peace and joy into my troubled soul;

My weary heart at last found rest;

My way was then made clear and plain to me,

And in it I did walk, until my tired feet

Were borne aloft, far up above this life,

Where I do rest from toil and strife.

Then let this be to you a beacon star, ·

To guide you onward o'er lifes ebbing tide,

Where you shall at the Master's feet
Find rest, and all the loved ones greet;—
Where parting shall be never known;—
Where God shall know and claim his own.

    Look up, poor fainting soul!
      No longer, then, repine;
    For earthly cares shall not disturb
      The peace that shall be thine.

    Thy future shall be brighter far
      Than earthly scenes can be,
    For in the heavens God will show
      His great love unto thee.

EARTH'S SORROWING ONES.

Think you their souls, filled with despair,
Shall ache throughout eternity?
As age on age rolls on, shall ceaseless pain be theirs?
Will God forget—will he disdain the cry
Of his erring children when they call for help?
Ah! no; but he'll forgive their comings short,—
Their sins which men remember still,
And count them o'er and o'er so many times,
'Till, had they their way, they'd pile up high,
Like mountains reaching to the sky,
Vast as oceans, rolling on in ceaseless tide,
From shore to shore expanding wide.
Well hath the poet said, in verse,
"Man's inhumanity to man
Makes countless thousands mourn."
So will it ever be 'till man his duty learns

Unto his brother.   Then shall he know as he is
    known,
And each his brother love as he himself is loved;
The lion with the lamb lie down; and

    Man, set free from sin and mortal strife,
    Shall find his name writ in the Book of Life;
    Then, upward rising, rising higher,
    Shall reach the mountain top of his desire.

PRAYER UNDER AFFLICTION.

My prayer is unto thee this day;
My thoughts do turn from earth away;
My weary soul would fain find rest,
But thou, O God! knoweth what is best.
Yes, I would in thy wisdom trust;
No longer for earth's comforts lust,
But give up all, and hope to find
Ease to my dark and troubled mind.
Shouldst thou still see my need,
And find it best my heart to bleed,
Be this my prayer and this my plea:
O God! be still a shield to me.

Why is the soul so burdened with care
While here on earth we stay?
Why filled with dark dispair

While passing thro' this wilderness?
Lift thy fainting spirit up,
And find a balm, a sure relief,
In every bitter cup.

INVOCATION.

Forgive, O Lord! the sins of each and every day
 While here on earth I stay.
Be near to me through every hour,
 And show to me thine own great power.
When thou dost see that I am weak,
 Make me lowly, contrite, meek;
And when the cares of life are past,
 Receive me to thyself at last.
To thy name shall then be given
 All the praise in earth and heaven.

ANGEL WHISPERS.

Come to me, thou bright, wing'd angels,
  Bringing light and sunshine near;
I am lonely and forsaken,
  For no loved one now is near.

I see a storm cloud in the distance.
  It fills my soul with dread affright.
See! oh, see! the storm approaches,
  And no loved one is in sight.

Hark! I hear a voice now saying,
  "Fear not; I am ever near—
Near, to comfort and sustain thee;
  Why shouldst thou, then, longer fear.

"Come to me, thou loved and cherished;
  Soon life's battles will be o'er;
Soon you'll view those scenes celestial
  On the bright, 'the shining shore.'"

HYMN.

"Oh! for a thousand tongues" to tell the wonders I
  have seen:

The matchless wisdom and the grace of our eternal
  King.

His wondrous power is ever seen, on earth and in
  the sky.

His goodness and his love we'll sing, and never,
  never die.

There is no death. The soul of man will ever jour-
  ney on

In happiness and joy, till freed from all its weary
  strife;

And as the soul is freed from sin and all its dark-
  ness blight,

Fresh joys shall open to its sight, and day shall
  banish night.

TO ONE IN SORROW.

O sorrowful soul! O weary heart!
Stung by many a poisoned dart,
Lift thy sad, sad eyes to heaven,
And unto you' shall then be given
A rich reward,—a treasure rare,
Of brightest gems beyond compare.
Then shall open to your sight
Visions pure and fair and bright,
Which shall be ever new to you.
Flowers whose fragrance shall endure,
Fountains of living water pure,
Streams, and lakes, and mountains high,
Reaching far above the sky;
The sun, the moon, and planets too,
As they their destined course pursue,—

You shall behold with rapturous gaze.
And while your soul is all ablaze
With joy supreme, and pure delight,
Eternal day shall banish all the weary night.

KNOW THYSELF.

Wouldst thou from sin be free?
Then upward look, and see
The heavens parted like a scroll,
Revealing unto thee thy naked soul,
Stripped of its tinseled covering,
Of all outside adorning;
Naked before thy God,
As Adam when taken from the sod.
Pause, then, and know thyself,
And quickly hie to remedy thy faults.

FEAR NOT.

Listen, listen! I can hear
　　Sweetest music in the air;
Silver harps with strings of gold,
　　Touched by angel fingers fair.

And the echo, soft and low,
　　Still is lingering in my ear;
As it floats upon the air,
　　Whispers gently, "Do not fear."

Angel voices seem to utter
　　Words of comfort, words of cheer;
And the anthem loud is ringing,
　　"Come up higher; do not fear.

Fear not, tho' thy weary footsteps
　　Seem to falter by the way;
Soon the pearly gates will open
　　Leading to eternal day.

ANGEL VOICES.

Yes, I hear the angels singing
  In the heavenly choirs above;
And their voices, sweetly blending,
  Tell of hope, and joy, and love.

And the music of their harp-strings
  Blend together in sweet accord;
As the notes are rising higher,
  No discordant sounds are heard.

Would that mortals, on the earth-plane,
  From the angel world would learn
To be loving, true and tender,—
  Not so cold, and hard, and stern.

Then would Earth and Heaven meet,
  And no longer should we see
Envy, hate and discord rampant,
  But all would dwell in unity.

TEARS.

There are tears, salt briny tears,
That fail to bring the heart
The comfort and the peace of mind
That God, the Father desires to give
Those whom he calls his own;
And then, again, there's tears
That cause the tender heart to bleed,
To sorrow, and to e'en distrust
The goodness of God's love:
But there are tears that cause the soul
To look still higher up, and see
God's hand in even tears,—
That fill the soul with thankfulness,
And peace in after years.
May God bless him or her who sees
The wisdom and omnipotence

Of Deity,—who, seeing, learns to kiss
The hand which chastens with the rod,
Not of his wrath, as some do say,
But of his love, his mercy too.
Oh! God, the Lord, is good,
And unto him shall praise be given,
Both now and evermore, amen.
Let the heavens echo with the shout,
As angels catch the glad refrain,
Until the vaulted arches ring
With one triumphal song.

When the white wing'd angel calleth for thee,
Wilt thou be ready, with nothing to fear?
When the pale boatman roweth thee o'er
The cold, silent river, the river of death,
Wilt shrink, or gladly respond to the call,
And hail, with delight, on the opposite brink,
The friends who stand waiting, stand ready to give
The kindest of greetings on the "evergreen shore"?

THE FUTURE.

Must I lay this body down,
And must I flee away?
Will my spirit, looking, looking down
On this poor form of clay,
Regret its loss, or e'er repine,
As I do upward soar?
Will earthly joys retard my flight?
Ah! no; no, never more,
For I have long desired to be
With loved ones gone before,
To see them as they now are seen;
To take their hand once more,
And con the lessons o'er again
We learned in days of yore;
To read again the story of
That olden time once more,
And see it in a golden light

THE FUTURE.

Not seen by us before.
Ah! yes; we then shall know
God's plans are wisest, best;
That if we put our trust in him,
He'll give us peace and rest.

———————

Sail on, and ever keep in view the light—
Tis even now in sight.
All hail! the glorious sun appears,
To banish night,
And cloudless shines eternal day,
That ne'er shall end in night.

THE BOOK OF LIFE.

There are minds, empty minds,
That they never will be filled,
Until they reach the other side of life,
Where they will find a page, all blank,
To fill with records of a former life.
Woe to him whose pages then shall teem,
With history of bad deeds done
While dwelling on the earthly plane.
Well for him if his name be writ
In God's own book, The Book of Life;
Well for him if no blot be found,
Nothing which needs to be erased,
So that its pages shall look clean and white—
Not here and there a crooked line
To straighten out or, worse, erase.
Oh! happy soul! to whom his God will say:

"Well done; come higher up,
And drink with me a sweeter cup—
Of nectar pure, of wine, fresh from the lees;
Eat, too, of fruitage from the trees;
Pluck from the ever-trailing vine,
And eat and drink new wine
'Till your soul shall fill with happiness
And overflow with bliss,
Your bosom thrill with purest joy,
While with the loved ones you employ
The hours in deeds of love,
And find true happiness above."

HYMN.

How shall we in the judgment stand?
　How meet thy holy face?
We who have sinned, and sinned oft,
　Would now our steps retrace.

We fein would fly where oft we've longed
　To find our welcome rest—
Where naught that hinders or makes afraid
　Can stir our peaceful breast—

Where sin and sorrow never come,
　To cause our hearts to bleed,
For God, the Father, them will bless,
　And supply our every need.

Oh! God, the Lord, is good to all
　Who seek to do his will;
And he will nevermore forsake,
　But will be near them still.

In darkest hours and sorrows sore
   His love will cheer them still,
And never shall their heartstrings break·
   While they his will fulfill.

PASSING AWAY.

Harken, harken! I can hear
Voices sweetly chanting clear;
Heavenly music in the air,
Luring me from worldly care.
I can here no longer stay,
For they beckon me away
To my heavenly home above,
Where all is peace, and joy, and love.
I must hasten to be gone,
My life's work is nearly done;
Fare thee well, my dearest friend,
All earthly joys are at an end.
Hark! I hear the angels call;
Farewell, farewell—all.

THE NEW BIRTH.

When the angelic hosts, advancing,
Meet a spirit freed from earth,
Loudly peal the bells of heaven
O'er the new immortal birth.

Angel voices join the chorus,
"Come up higher! Do not fear,"
While the vaulted arch of heaven
Rings the echo loud and clear.

"Come up higher!" and the spirit,
Responding gladly to the call,
Upward rising, still advancing,
Meets the Lord, the God of all.

PART II.

CHRISTMAS.

Beautiful day that God to us has given
To win our hearts from earth to heaven!
How our souls do swell with joy
While we our busy hands employ
In kindly deeds to others wrought
As the poor this day are sought,
And we supply their many needs,
Their hearts make glad by kindly deeds,
Their wants relieve, their sorrows heal,
And thus upon their hearts do seal
The impress of God's tender love.
Akin to that which reigns above,
His tender hand is ever laid
On all the creatures he has made,
However lowly be their lot,
Whether they dwell in hut or cot,

God's care is all the same;
Nor does he e'er the lowly blame.
Methinks I hear the angelic choir
Swelling the anthem loud and clear,
"Glory to God who dwells on high,
Who unto us is ever nigh,
For he to us has freely given
A passport into heaven.
Not through the death of his dear son,
Not thro' his sufferings we have won,
But by his grace and love,
By good deeds done beneath above,
While dwelling on the earthly plane,
Which God doth not disdain.
His grace he ever will bestow
On all who ask who seek to know
His own good gracious will.
He will be ever 'round them still
Who for others live and not for self,
Who seek not earthly goods or pelf.

Blessed, thrice blessed he
Who loves his kind, and who agree,
Who seek some good to do to all,
Whether they be great or small,
Thereby rising higher in the scale of life,
'Till they do reach eternal life,
Where ever bloom the flowers bright,
Filling the soul with pure delight;
Where trees immortal, ever green,
By gladsome spirits shall be seen.
Oh! the depths of the Father's love
Is kin to that which reigns above.
It knows no change, nor can it die
When the heart is touched thereby;
When the lips are touched by holy fire,
Fresh from God's altar, then angel lyres
Shall strike glad notes of praise
To him who hath no end of days,
And man shall catch the glad refrain.
"There's no more death or pain;

Nothing shall hurt or make afraid
In all my holy mount," 'tis said.
Angel voices, too, shall swell the strain,
"We immortal joys have gained."
Earth with triumphant shout shall sing,
While all to God their offerings bring,
And lay them at Jehovah's feet,
An offering fit, and pure, and mete.

MY BLOSSOM.

If I do hold within my hand
  A blossom sweet and rare,
Shall I not keep it near my heart,
  And nurture it with care?

If that blossom fail to yield
  To me a rich return
For all the care bestowed on it,
  And I am called to mourn;

If it should wither in my grasp,
  Its leaves should fade away,
And I could gather naught but thorns,
  All else should then decay,

Must I sit down in gloomy doubt
  And fail to try again?
Oh! rather let me, with my tears,
  Bring back its life again.

Should my tears then fail to bring
    My blossom back to me,
Oh! may it bloom in Heaven above,
    Through vast eternity.

Then may I turn where never fade
    The sunset or the flowers;
Where tender plants are nurtured still,
    Refreshed by balmy showers;

Where angel bands do ever keep
    Their watch-care over all,
The high, the low, the rich, the poor,
    Alike the great and small.

AFTER THE NIGHT THE MORNING DAWNETH.

Weary, weary is the day, waiting for the coming May;

Sad and darksome is the night, for my heart is full of blight;

Slowly roll the lagging hours, waiting for the April showers.

Cease, oh cease, my weary heart, in worldly cares to take a part!

Surely there must come some rest, but thou, O God, knoweth what is best.

Trust in him, O troubled soul, you will surely win the goal;

You will in the future find God, the Father, to be kind;

That which now to you looks dark you will find a radiant spark

Of light divine, of purest ray, that will end in perfect day.

Then look up and be content; no longer droop in discontent.

Be firm in duty; some good deed may many others
   lead.

Onward, upward, thro' earthly strife, unto an eternal
   life.

Then shall new beauties be revealed that shall o'er
   your spirit steal,

Unknown to you before. You shall learn of spirit
   lore,

A language pure and undefiled as cometh from a lit-
   tle child;

You the stars shall read in language strange and
   new;

And as you fly through ether space, and you your
   course retrace,

You shall take up this glad refrain: My life was
   not, not all in vain.

    You've drank the bitter cup of life,

      E'en to its bitter dregs;

    And unto you shall now be given

      A passport into heaven.

WRITTEN

**TO MY ESTEEMED FRIEND, MISS A. B.,
DURING A SEVERE ILLNESS.**

Why shouldst thou fear to cross the river?
'Tis but a narrow stream, and on the
Other side are pleasures evermore.
Then let thy frail bark glide gently o'er,
And find thy secret longings gratified;
Nay, more—find friends and happiness
Beyond the ken of mortal mind.
Earth has not brought contentment;
Pass over, then, and reach the goal immortal.

FROM A SPIRIT FRIEND.

Who is ever about to lead and guide
If thou wouldst only heed.
Shut not up thy soul against the truth.
Close not the portals when angels seek to enter.

SONG.

I'll come to thee in the morning, love,
 I'll come to thee at night;
I'll come to the whenever, love,
 Thou deemest best and right.

And we will happy be, love,
 As in the olden time;
And we will of the past speak,
 In good old-fashioned rhyme.

We'll banish all the past, love,
 That brings to us a sigh;
We'll only at the bright side look,
 And never say good bye.

TO A STRANGER.

ON BEING ASKED TO WRITE IN HER ALBUM.

You asked me to write in your album—
The reason I cannot tell.
Shall it be prose or poem,
Or will either suit you well?
As I am rather more prosy
Than given to making rhymes,
Will bid you a pleasant good morning,
Wishing you merrier, happier times.

TO THE SAME.

Should your eye e'er rest on these few lines,
Turn not to other pages, seeking
From friendships urn to draw sweet consolation,
But give to me a passing thought—if only one,

And with it add a blessing.
As you do give so may you receive,
Until life's cup shall fill and overflow
With purest joy and happiness combined.

WRITTEN TO A FRIEND.

Think of me when the sun is shining,
   Bathing the earth in light;
Think of me when the stars are gleaming
   Pure and bright;
Think of me when the flowers are blooming
   Sweet and gay;
Think of me both now and ever,
   Think of me alway.

SPRING.

Spring time is coming, coming, coming,
 And our hearts are full of glee
As the music of the birdling
 Floats upon the summer breeze;

And the beauty of the flowers
 Tell us God is ever nigh—
Speak to us of heavenly beauty
 As their fragrance fills the air.

Shrub and flower, plant and tree,
 All in beauteous harmony,
Speak the power of God eternal—
 Speak to us of Deity—

Tell us God is good to all—
 Tell us he is love and truth—
Tell us to be like unto him,
 That we may dwell in unity.

M A Y.

O fairy, fairy, fairy day!
Welcome, welcome first of May,
Time of lovely buds and flowers,
Sweetest month in fairy bowers.
We would hail the Queen of days—
Crown thee with devinest rays.
Would thy days did number more;
Would we could forever store,
Ever, ever, evermore,
All the sweets in days of yore,
And to thee the offering bring,
Sweetest, sweetest month of spring.

HOPE.

Oh! the beautiful, beautiful, balmy air
Seems to rob my heart of care;
The beautiful sun, the beautiful trees,
As they put forth their bright green leaves,
Fill my radiant soul with light,
Banishing all the weary night.
As I lift up my eyes to heaven,
New aspirations to me are given;
I take up anew the burden of life,
Again go out where sin and strife
Can no more cause my heart to bleed.
As I look to God to supply my need,
Looking beyond this vale of tears,
Hoping that in the coming years
Somewhere God will dry my tears

And make the trials so hard to endure
To form a crown of jewels pure
That shall encircle my weary head
When I am numbered with the dead.

DISAPPOINTMENT.

Whither away, whither away, my fair young maid?
Art looking for lilies or roses under the shade?
The flowers are blooming all sweet and gay
In this the beautiful month of May;
Dost seek for thy lover, my sweet young maid,
Walking up and down thro' the flowery glade?
'Tis useless to seek him.   He has left thee for good;
Left thee because thou wert misunderstood.
Many more have done the same thing, fair girl,
In hunting the diamond overlooked the fair pearl.

TO A LOVED ONE.

Oh, how I loved thy raven hair!
Thy bright black eyes, thy form so fair!
Thy graceful step, thy modest mien:
Thou seemest covered with silver sheen.
Little thought we then so soon to part,
One to be left with broken heart;
But that which seemed to us, my dear,
So cruel and so hard to bear
Was needed by us both, my love,
To fit us for our home above.

WRITTEN IN A FRIEND'S ALBUM.

Let this to you a token be of friendship true,
    Although in words unspoken;
And may the links in memory's chain
    For us remain unbroken.

THE HUNTER'S SONG.

I come, I come from my forest home,
    Among the tall oak trees,
Where the foliage green is ever seen,
    Stirred by the morning breeze.

My haunts are far from the ken of man,
    My footsteps light and free
As I spring across the rocky cliffs
    Jutting far over the sea.

Oh! my life it is a merry one,
    As I hunt the bounding stag,
As I roam the forest in search of game,
    Springing from craig to craig.

Ah! who would barter his freedom away,
    Who would give in exchange
His forest home, his freedom from care,
    For a cottage or a grange.

THE COMING VICTORY.

E'en now I hear a shout
Come up on every hand:
"Alcohol must be banished
From this our own loved land!"

All around are rising,
And to the rescue come;
Our valiant sons and brothers,
Who say: "It shall be done.

The demon shall be vanquished,
For we put our trust in God,
And he will surely save us,
Tho' chastened by his rod."

What is the sound I hear?
"No license!" is the cry.
"We'll fight the monster Alcohol,
And conquer tho' we die.

We will poll our votes,
While our sisters cheer us on;
We'll save our fellow brother
From the dread effects of rum."

I hear it in the distance;
It now is nearer come;
Higher yet the shout goes up,
And down will go the rum.

The battle's nearly over,
The victory'll soon be won;
We'll shout aloud, Hosannah!
Hallelujah! we have won.

SONG.

I love to hunt the bounding stag;
  I love to hunt the deer;
I love to cross the pearly streams,
  So rippling and so clear.

I love to roam the forest through,
  And through the woods so wild;
I love to turn my thoughts away
  From this sad world awhile.

I love to hear the whisper of
  Sweet music 'mong the pines;
I love to feel that God is near
  In every whistling wind.

I love to hear the rain-drops fall;
  To see the lightings flash;
I love to see the dark clouds meet,
  And hear the thunder crash.

Oh! yes; I love the flowers too,
  So sweet, and yet so mild;
I love the birds and their sweet notes,
  They cheer my heart the while.

I've wandered òver all the earth,
  And seen its cheats and wile;
I've sailed o'er the ocean wide .
  Full many a weary mile.

Yes, I have wandered up and down
  Throughout this weary world,
But I have found no diamond,
  Or any goodly pearl.

ALL NATURE PRAISES GOD.

When the summer showers fall upon the earth,
And the tiny dew-drop gives the flowers birth,
Then our Heavenly Father fills our hearts with mirth,
Sends his choicest blessings over all the earth.
The tiny little violet opens her eyes of blue
When the sun is shining, sips the morning dew
As she so modestly lifts her little head,
Peeping out from under her mossy-covered bed.
And the little birdling sings his happy song,
As he flits from bough to bough in the summer morn,
Chirping so merrily all the live-long day,
Giving all the praise to God in his merry lay.
The tall and mighty oak from the acorn springing,
With the tender ivy round its branches clinging,
Proudly waves its branches before the swaying wind,
Seeming to boast itself the noblest of its kind.
Pearly stream, and brooklet running swiftly by,

Falls into the ocean without e'en a sigh,

As the sea engulfs them in its stormy breast,

Mingling with the waters beneath its snowy crest.

All nature praises God; the earth, the sea, the sky,

All speak the great Creator to be forever nigh.

Then why should man, his noblest work, not give
    him all the praise—

Not mourning go, and sorrowing, throughout his
    length of days.

THE END.